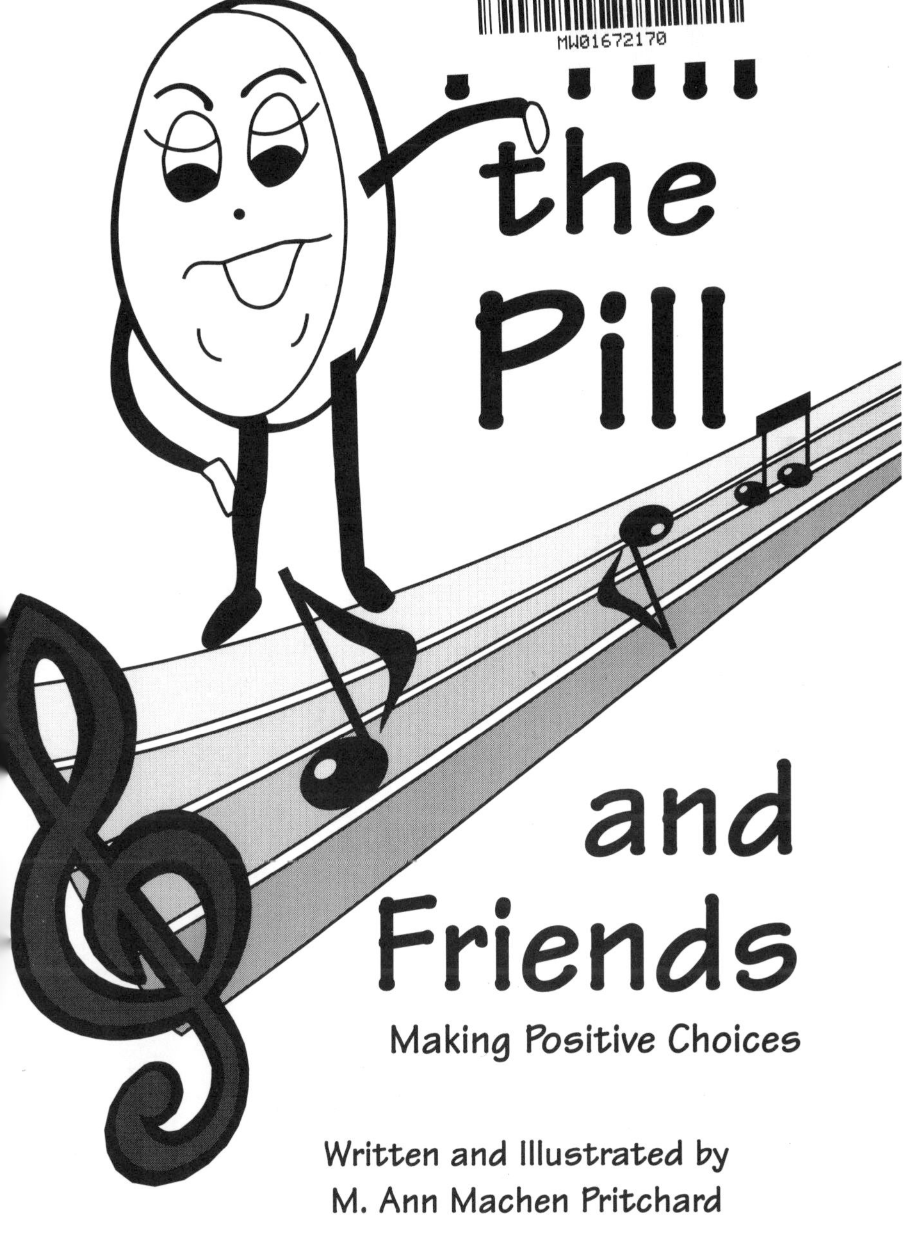

the Pill and Friends

Making Positive Choices

Written and Illustrated by
M. Ann Machen Pritchard

PHIL THE PILL

Phil the Pill, a cartoon character created by M. Ann Machen Pritchard.

Phil's goal is to encourage kids to stay in school, read, and make positive choices in life.

MAMP Creations
P.O. Box 4253
Hopkins, MN 55343
952-938-9320

Editor: Sequoya Nelson

ISBN 0-9772210-0-8

Printed in the United States of America

This book is dedicated in memory
of my Mom, Ida Ola Mae (Green) Machen
and my Dad, Rev. M. David Machen, Sr.,
who always taught me to work hard,
be a good person and
make positive choices in life.

Acknowledgments

I would like to take this time to say thank you to everyone who was an inspiration in my life to write this book.

First, I would like to thank God for giving me strength.
Also my parents, the late Rev. M. David Machen, Sr. and Ida Ola Mae (Green) Machen.

I would like to say thank you to my children, Sequoya and Danny.
My grandchildren, Montayia, Mark, Jonathan and Lexcia.
You all are a joy to me.

I would like to say thank you to my sisters, Dorcas and Pearl.
You are sensational.

Also, thank you to Lewis Songer, Dee Hobbie, Nancy Fish and Laurie Etchen and many other family and friends that believed in me. Thanks to you all.

Contents

Hello, my name is Phil the Pill. I want to tell you some little stories about my friends. Some days my friends may be happy and some days my friends may be sad. But they all learn how to have fun and make positive choices in life.

Phil the Pill's friends

Dan is a grumpy character who doesn't care much about anything.

Bill is a soft-spoken, nice character who helps keep his friend, Dan, in line.

Val made a change in her life, and spends her time motivating others.

Jill is Phil the Pill's assistant.
She uses her melodic voice to encourage kids to make positive choices in life.

Little Dan

is a child with many

questions and

curiosities.

He is searching

for answers.

Dan Talks It Out

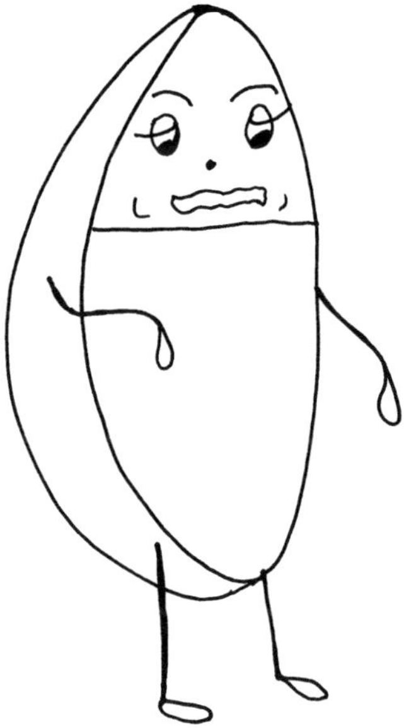

I have a good friend who lives in Chicago. His name is Bill. He is a very nice person. Bill likes to make people laugh. He laughs every day. He says that when you laugh, you can feel better if you are feeling sad.

Dan is very grumpy today.

“What is wrong with you, Dan?” asked Bill.

“Who cares? Who wants to know? I don’t care,” Dan answered.

“Maybe I can help you feel better,” Bill offered.

"Nothing seemed to go the right way for me today," said Dan. "I even tried to cook my dinner and messed it up. I give up. Maybe today I should just sit at home and not do anything."

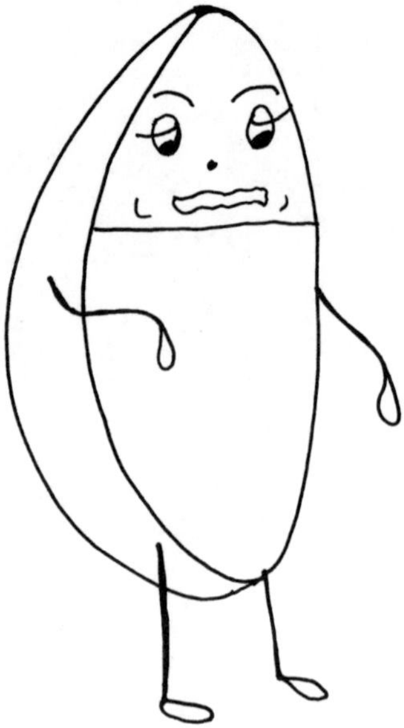

"I know what you could do today," said Bill. "You could make a peanut butter and jelly sandwich for dinner. It would be hard to mess that up, Ha Ha!" Bill laughed.

"Come on, Bill, stop making fun of me," replied Dan. "I am having a bad day today."

"Don't be blue, Dan," said Bill. "I will help you. Just close your eyes and think about good, fun things. Then laugh as loud as you can and you can feel better. Just give it a try."

"OK," said Dan. "Ha Ha Ha. Ha Ha Ha! Hey, thanks but it is not working for me. I still feel blue."

“Dan, do you want to talk about what is bothering you today?” asked Bill.

“No, No, No!” replied Dan. “Just leave me alone.”

“I know what to do,” said Bill. “I’ll get Val to come and sing you a song.”

"Hello, Dan. How are you doing?" asked Val.

"I feel down today, but I don't need anyone or anything. Today has been all messed up for me," Dan replied.

"Do you want to talk about why you think today is all messed up for you?" asked Val.

"No, No, No!" Dan exclaimed.

"Well, let's get Phil to come here so we can sing a song for you. Hey Phil! Dan needs us to sing a song so he can feel better today."

"I know, we can sing ***Talk It Out,*** " said Phil. "Let's get Jill to help us."

Phil, Val and Jill sang to Dan.

"You've got to talk it out . . .
Then walk it out.
Don't keep it bottled up inside of you.
If you have an issue . . .
It's OK to use a tissue . . .
To wipe away your tears of blue."

Talk It Out

words and music by:
M. Ann Machen Pritchard

March tempo

"Hey, do you mean it's OK if I feel bad that I can talk about it? I should not keep it bottled up inside of me, right?" asked Dan.

"Right," they replied.

"You will be OK, Dan," said Phil. "You need to calm down. Then you can talk about what ever is making you sad. You can talk to your Mom or Dad. Maybe your teacher, a friend, or if you have a brother or sister, you can talk to any of them. We all care about you and want you to have a happy day."

Reading is Intriguing

"Have you read your story yet, Little Dan?" asked Phil.

"No, I played all day and totally forgot about it. Why do I have to read?" asked Little Dan.

"If you can read, you will be able to help others. If you read, you will be able to get a good job when you grow up. You can succeed in whatever you decide that you want to be in life," Phil answered.

“Dan, there is a little song you can sing to help you think about why you should learn how to read,” said Phil. “It goes like this. . .”

"Reading is intriguing . . .
Reading will take you on a great adventure
        and educate you for success . . .
in whatever you may venture.
        Reading will help your mind grow . . .
to understand whatever you want to know.
Learn how to read so you will succeed."

Reading Is Intriguing

words and music by:
M. Ann Machen Pritchard

Play Responsibly and Get Your Rest

"I would like to go out and play in the park today. It will be lots of fun," said Little Dan. "But I have to remember something that Phil told me about going to the park.
Oh no! I forgot what he told me to do!
I will ask Jill. She will know what to do."

"Hello, Jill," said Little Dan. "I can't remember what Phil told me about going to the park. Can you tell me what I should do?"

Jill answered, "I will sing a little song that may help you to remember. It is a song about a little boy named Mark. Hmmm."

"I know a little boy named Mark . . .
Who loves to go to the park.
To play and run . . .
Just have lots of fun . . .
But he must be home before dark.

He loves to swing . . .
and see everything . . .
He loves to slide . . .
because it's a real cool ride . . .
But he must be home before dark.
He must be home before dark."

"Always remember when you go to the park, you must be home before dark."

A Little Boy Named Mark

words and music by:
M. Ann Machen Pritchard

Lively

Spoken: Always remember, when you go to the park, you must be home before dark.

"Now do you remember what you are supposed to do, Little Dan?" asked Jill.

"Yes, I must be home before dark, right?" Little Dan replied.

"That's right," said Jill.

“I love that song, Jill,” said Little Dan. “Please sing me another one. Sing one about going to sleep. Sometimes I have a hard time going to sleep. It might help me if you sing me a song.”

“OK”, said Jill.

"Go to sleep . . .you don't have to weep.
Just go to sleep . . . and don't even peep.
You need your rest so you can be your best.
Every day . . . I say . . .
It's the best way."

"Get plenty of rest so you can be your best."

Go To Sleep

Words and music by:
M. Ann Machen Pritchard

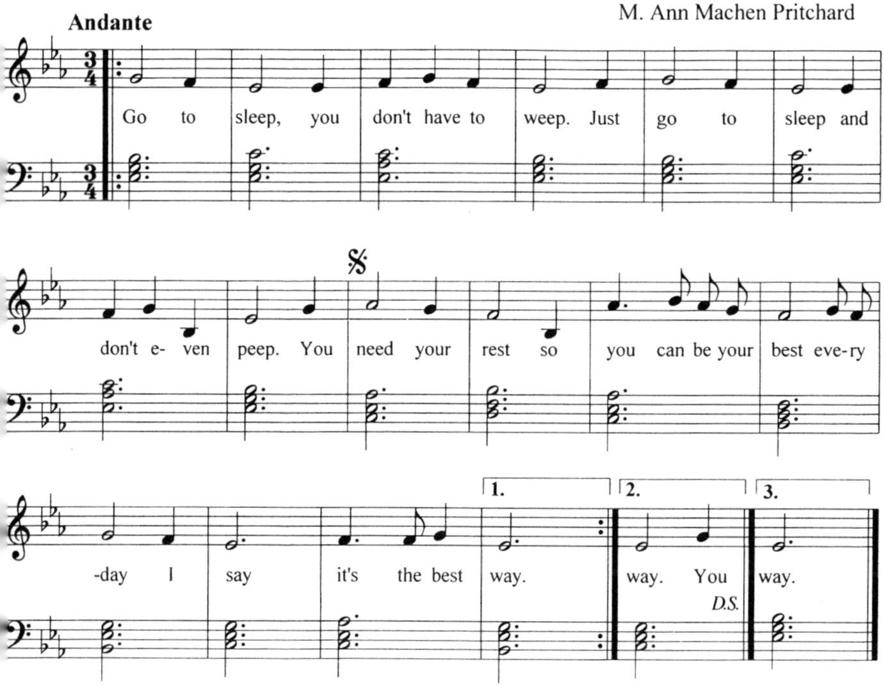

spoken: Get plenty of rest so you can be your best!

"Thank you, Jill," said Little Dan. "Now I know how important it is to learn how to read and get plenty of rest so I can be my best. I will be home before dark when I go out to play with my friends. I know that I will be whatever I want to be when I grow up. Why?

Because I will stay in school, I will make positive choices in life and I will be a big success!"

Sing-a-Long

"Hey everybody, I want to sing a song for you," said Phil. "Will you sing along with me?"

Bill, Dan, Val, Jill and Little Dan came rushing into the room to help Phil sing a song.

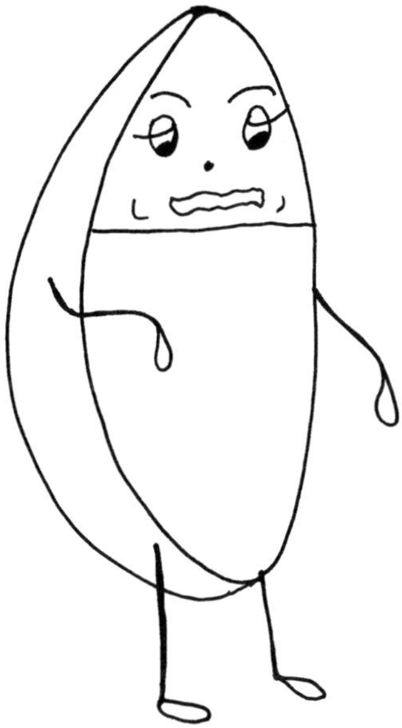

“What are we going to sing?” asked Bill.

"I will sing! La La La," sang Dan.

“No, I will sing,” said Val. “Stop complaining, I'm a cook in training! Stop complaining, I'm a cook in training!”

"Wait a minute, wait just a minute!" shouted Little Dan. "I will sing a song, just sing with Phil and me."

“OK, OK, everyone. Let’s get started,” said Jill. “We are going to sing a song that you all will enjoy. Ready? One, two, three, let’s sing!”

"I'm sweet 'n' neat with 2 little feet . . .
I'll run and play and grow up someday.
When I grow up . . . you will see . . .
I will be whatever I want to be.
I will be whatever I want to be."

*"I will be a Teacher or I will be a Preacher . . .
I will be whatever I want to be."*

"I will be a Doctor or I will be a Lawyer . . .
I will be whatever I want to be."

"I'm sweet 'n' neat with 2 little feet . . .
I'll run and play and grow up someday.
When I grow up . . . you will see . . .
I will be whatever I want to be.
I will be whatever I want to be."

"I will be a Plumber or I will be a Drummer . . .
I will be whatever I want to be."

*"I will be a Policeman or I will be a Fireman . . .
I will be whatever I want to be."*

"I'm sweet 'n' neat with 2 little feet . . .
I'll run and play and grow up someday.
When I grow up . . . you will see . . .
I will be whatever I want to be.
I will be whatever I want to be."

"I will be a Ballerina
or the Mayor of Pasadena . . .
I will be whatever I want to be."

"I will be a Nurse
or I will sing another verse . . .
I will be whatever I want to be."

"I'm sweet 'n' neat with 2 little feet . . .
I'll run and play and grow up someday.
When I grow up . . . you will see . . .
I will be whatever I want to be.
I will be whatever I want to be."

I'm Sweet 'N' Neat With 2 Little Feet

Words and music by:
M. Ann Machen Pritchard

"I really love that song, Phil," said Little Dan. "I will think about what I want to be when I grow up, and get my education so I will succeed. Thanks for helping me."

"That is great," Phil replied. "Going to school is really cool."

The End

The End

ABOUT THE AUTHOR

Ann (Machen) Pritchard was born in Elizabethton, Tennessee, one of 16 children.
In her hometown area she is known as a former actress, model, stage make-up artist and singer.

After observing many trials and tribulations throughout her life, she was inspired to encourage people of all ages to make positive choices.
The choice that Ann made for her life led to the creation of the cartoon characters, Phil the Pill and Friends. Her passion and mission is to encourage everyone that it is not the end of the world when things don't always go our way.
She strongly believes that if we learn to make positive choices at an early age, we can get through more difficult challenges now and later in life.